# ACTIVITY BANK

# Smoking

Gerald Beales

# Contents

How to use this book     3

Introduction     3

*Activity*

| | | |
|---|---|---|
| 1 | Poisonous smoke | 4 |
| 2 | Keeping fit – looking good | 6 |
| 3 | Who are you kidding? | 8 |
| 4 | Thinking ahead | 10 |
| 5 | Counting the cost | 12 |
| 6 | An irritating habit | 14 |
| 7 | A smoker in the family | 16 |
| 8 | No smoking! | 18 |
| 9 | How many young people smoke? | 20 |
| 10 | Good for your image? | 22 |
| 11 | Fooled by the ads | 24 |
| 12 | Should ads be banned? | 26 |

*Activity*

| | | |
|---|---|---|
| 13 | Going along with the crowd | 28 |
| 14 | Hooked on tobacco | 30 |
| 15 | Breaking the habit | 32 |
| 16 | Who needs cigarettes? | 34 |
| 17 | How to quit | 36 |
| 18 | Illegal sales | 38 |
| 19 | Making up your own mind | 40 |
| | Smoking Fact Sheets | 42 |
| | References and resources | 47 |
| | Skills matrix | 48 |

---

Folens allows photocopying of pages marked 'copiable page' for educational use, providing that this use is within the confines of the purchasing institution. Copiable pages should not be declared in any return in respect of any photocopying licence.

Folens books are protected by international copyright laws. All rights are reserved. The copyright of all materials in this book, except where otherwise stated, remains the property of the publisher and author. No part of this publication may be reproduced, stored in a retrieval system, or transmitted, in any form or by any means, for whatever purpose, without the written permission of Folens Limited.

This resource may be used in a variety of ways. However, it is not intended that teachers or children should write directly into the book itself.

Gerald Beales hereby asserts his moral right to be identified as the author of this work in accordance with the Copyright, Designs and Patents Act 1988.

Editor: Sue Harmes
Layout artist: Patricia Hollingsworth
Illustrations: Charmaine Peters

© 2000 Folens Limited, on behalf of the authors.

Every effort has been made to contact copyright holders of material used in this book. If any have been overlooked, we will be pleased to make any necessary arrangements.

First published 2000 by Folens Limited, Dunstable and Dublin.

Folens Limited, Albert House, Apex Business Centre, Boscombe Road, Dunstable, LU5 4RL, England.

ISBN 1 86202 567-3

Printed in Singapore at Craft Print.

# How to use this book

There are 19 activities contained within this book. Each one has a teacher instruction page and a pupil activity page. The activities can be completed in short time slots or extended into longer periods, depending on the length of time you have available. They can also be differentiated to suit the needs of less able pupils. The activities can be presented in any order and you do not have to work your way right through the book. A matrix on page 48 provides a useful summary of, and reference to, the skills that students will learn through each activity, but we do recommend that Activity 1 is presented as the starting point of your series of lessons and Activity 19 at the end. The Smoking Fact Sheets also provide a useful resource for teachers to enhance the activities.

Most of the activities in this book need few materials or resources other than copies of the activity sheet, paper and pens. They are designed to keep the teacher's workload to a minimum beyond planning how each activity will be carried out in the classroom. Most are designed so that pupils can work individually, in pairs or in small groups, depending on the teacher's preference. We recommend a balance of whole class, small group and individual work to provide pupils with plenty of opportunity to express their views, to listen and to try to understand the views of others and to develop communication and social skills.

The aims and expected outcomes of each activity are clearly indicated and the format for all activities is consistent to enable you quickly to feel comfortable and familiar with the style. All the information a teacher needs is contained here, not only to present the lesson confidently but also to answer most questions that arise.

This book will help to meet both the requirements of OFSTED regarding moral and social guidance, and the DfEE's Framework for PSHE.

# Introduction

At a time when tolerance to smoking is decreasing among adults, current statistics show that smoking among young people is still on the increase, especially among girls. That it remains a mainstream PSHE topic in schools today is therefore particularly significant.

Recent Government initiatives to introduce a total ban on cigarette advertising indicate the high profile given to the threat to health posed by smoking. Schools will be expected to follow this lead in supplying the facts that may encourage a reversal in the current trends.

This book aims to supply the hard facts about smoking. It begins by examining the physical damage caused (including that caused by passive smoking and smoking during pregnancy). It considers other key areas such as the reasons why young people start the habit, the legal and economic implications, the causes of addiction and ways of giving it up.

Pupils will be required to use knowledge and understanding as they assess the key social, moral and health implications of smoking. By the end of the course they will be equipped to take responsibility for their own health and to make confident decisions in respect of these issues.

Activity 1 – Teacher's notes

# Poisonous smoke

*Recognising how tobacco smoke damages the body*

## AIMS

To encourage young people to be aware that pollutants such as cigarette smoke can harm physical organisms.

### Teaching Points

*Materials needed*
Health Education Authority publications, and leaflets from medical centres, pharmacies and supermarkets.

- Tobacco smoke contains thousands of chemicals. Many of these chemicals are harmful to the human body.
- Irritants in tobacco smoke destroy the tiny hairs in the air passages that normally trap dirt and germs. As a result, dirt and germs are able to travel into the lungs and accumulate there.
- Tar is a black, sticky substance that collects in the lungs. It contains products that are known to cause cancer. Even so-called 'low-tar' cigarettes are dangerous.
- Carbon monoxide, present in all cigarette smoke, is a poisonous gas that reduces the blood's ability to transport oxygen around the body. Oxygen is needed to build cells and convert food into energy.
- Nicotine is a powerful drug that affects the brain and heart.
- Smoking accelerates the natural ageing process of the blood vessels, damaging their smooth inner lining. The blood carried inside this is then more likely to form clots. When the blood supply to the brain or heart is blocked, a stroke or heart attack results.
- It is easy to ignore what goes on under our skin because we cannot see it.

## USING THE ACTIVITY SHEET

**The focus of the activity involves imagining the interior of the body and picturing the damage caused by smoking.**

**Step 1** Hand out copies of Smoking Fact Sheet 1. Collect and display reference materials that contain information on the constituents of tobacco smoke, how they travel into the body via the respiratory and circulatory systems, and their effects on health.

**Step 2** Ask the pupils to describe events that have made them aware of what was going on inside their bodies. List the events on the board and ask the pupils to feed back their observations.

**Step 3** Ask the pupils to complete the activity sheet, imagining the changes caused to the body by smoking. Ask them to describe and draw the damage.

**Step 4** In a plenary session, ask individual pupils to present their reports to the class. Write on the board the key words pupils use to describe the internal condition of smokers and non-smokers. Ask them to grade the types of damage in order of severity.

### Extension Activities

- Ask pupils to research the history of how tobacco was first discovered. They might present it in writing or as a cartoon for classroom display.

### Outcomes

- An increased understanding of the effects of smoking on the body's inner workings.
- An increased understanding of the health effects of smoking.
- The development of presentation skills.

**Activity Sheet 1**

# Poisonous smoke

Imagine that you have been shrunk extremely small so that you can travel in a special capsule inside the body of a smoker to the heart and other parts of the body. Draw some of the damage caused.

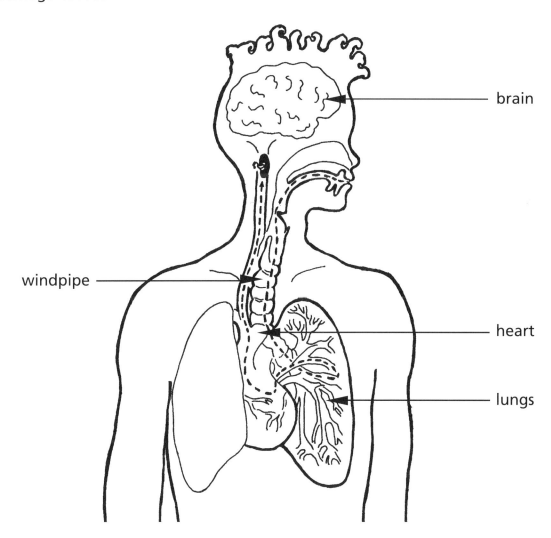

Now think of five words which best describe the condition of a smoker's air passages or lungs.

_____   _____   _____   _____   _____

Think of five more words which best describe the condition of a smoker's blood vessels.

_____   _____   _____   _____   _____

Finally, write down some words which apply to the same parts of a non-smoker.

_____

© Folens (copiable page)     ACTIVITY BANK: *Smoking*

Activity 2 – Teacher's notes

# Keeping fit – looking good

*Considering the more immediate and 'visible' effects of smoking*

## AIMS

To show how smoking can have immediate effects on young people, resulting in loss of fitness and attractiveness.

### Teaching Points

- Cancer and heart disease may take years to develop in a smoker, but other harmful effects can show up relatively quickly when a young person starts to smoke.
- Smokers soon become more prone to coughs and chest infections. In comparison with non-smokers, they may have more days when they feel unwell and may not enjoy life to the full.
- Because tobacco reduces the body's ability to deliver the oxygen that fuels muscles, young smokers become less fit and find they get out of breath more quickly.
- The chemicals in cigarette smoke also cause some unpleasant odours, affecting clothes and breath.
- Smoking harms the skin. It restricts the flow of blood to skin layers, causing them to wrinkle and age more quickly. Prolonged smoking also causes discolouration to the fingers, fingernails and teeth.
- When considering whether or not to smoke, young people may be more influenced by the 'visible' short-term effects than by the longer-term health risks.

## USING THE ACTIVITY SHEET

**The focus of the activity is to allow pupils to consider the short-term implications of smoking for people like themselves.**

**Step 1** Hand out Smoking Fact Sheet 2 on the harmful short-term effects of smoking. Make a class list of the effects in order of severity and then in order of probability. Ask the class if they can think of any unwanted consequences of these for young smokers (e.g. losing friendships because they smell of smoke).

**Step 2** Invite the pupils to describe what young smokers think are the benefits of smoking. Encourage them to think of as many benefits as possible. Write these good and bad effects on the board. Hand out copies of the activity sheet.

**Step 3** Ask for volunteers to act out a disco scenario in which some of the young people are smokers. The rest of the class can stop the action at any point and decide what the actors should say and do next. Remind them of all the good and bad effects listed on the board. Ask them to complete the first part of the activity sheet.

**Step 4** At the end of the scene, ask the class to discuss the pros and cons of smoking for each of the characters portrayed. Then ask them to complete the second part of the activity sheet. Hold a class vote on whether or not the pupils think that smoking is worthwhile.

### Extension Activities

- Ask pupils to design a poster that shows the effects that smoking can have on young people.
- Ask pupils to imagine that they are the coaches of a sports team who have just discovered that one of their players smokes. What do they say to that player?

### Outcomes

- A greater understanding of short-term negative effects of smoking.
- The development of evaluation skills in assessing whether the negative effects outweigh any immediate benefits of smoking.

**Activity Sheet 2**

# Keeping fit – looking good

Paul and Sian both smoke; their friends Hasan and Sophie do not.

Imagine a scene at a disco where Paul and Sian are trying to impress each other by smoking and their friends are trying to persuade them against it.

What happens next? Act out the next part of the scene.

1. Think about the people in the disco who were smokers. How did their smoking affect them? How good a time did they have?

   _____
   _____
   _____

   How did other people at the disco react to them?

   _____
   _____

2. Make a list of the ways in which some of the young people may have had more fun because they smoked. Make a second list of the ways in which their smoking may have made them have less fun.

| more fun | less fun |
| --- | --- |
| _____ | _____ |
| _____ | _____ |
| _____ | _____ |
| _____ | _____ |
| _____ | _____ |

Make a list of the pros and cons of smoking.

_____
_____
_____
_____

© Folens (copiable page)     ACTIVITY BANK: *Smoking*

Activity 3 – Teacher's notes

# Who are you kidding?

*How smokers can avoid facing the facts*

## AIMS

To provide knowledge of some of the psychological devices people may use to hide the unpleasant facts about smoking from themselves.

### Teaching Points

- Young people thinking of starting smoking are confronted by messages about the harmful effects of tobacco from several different sources. For example, the Government requires tobacco companies to put health warnings on cigarette packets.
- Although most children and adults may be affected by such messages, some use a variety of psychological devices to shut out unpleasant facts about smoking.
- Smokers' peer groups can support and reinforce each other in the use of such devices.
- If young people are to be enabled to make rational and informed decisions about smoking, they must be equipped to recognise and challenge such use of psychological devices.

## USING THE ACTIVITY SHEET

The focus of the activity is to provide an opportunity to recognise and respond to some of the psychological devices used by smokers.

**Step 1** Ask the class what kind of things they have heard smokers say in order to show that their smoking is safe (e.g. 'it won't happen to me', 'my uncle smoked all his life and lived until he was 90', 'it hasn't been proved that smoking causes cancer'). Write them on the board.

**Step 2** Ask the pupils to complete the first part of the activity sheet. It may also be useful to hand out copies of Smoking Fact Sheets 1 and 2 for reference.

**Step 3** Split the class into pairs or small groups and ask them to decide which of the patient's and doctor's arguments are facts and which are opinions. They then mark their facts '+' or '-' to denote support or opposition for smoking and decide whose argument has won.

**Step 4** Ask the pupils to complete the second part of the activity sheet.

**Step 5** Ask the pupils to report their results to the rest of the class. Did anyone think of any other ways that smokers might deceive themselves, in addition to those already on the board? Ask the class how sensible the smoker's answers were. Why do they think smokers ignore the existence of undesirable facts?

### Extension Activities

- Ask pupils to check and compare the different Government health warnings that appear on cigarette packets. How effective do they think these warnings are and why?
- The class could think of some other health warnings that would be effective for young people.

### Outcomes

- A greater understanding of the psychological devices young people may use to avoid facing the facts about smoking.
- A reduced likelihood that young people will use such devices in their own decision making on smoking.

**Activity Sheet 3**

# Who are you kidding?

Imagine a scene between a doctor and a patient. The patient is a smoker who gets out of breath easily and has a cough which won't go away. The doctor tries to persuade the patient to stop smoking, by explaining the health risks.

1. In the speech bubbles, write down:
   - Five reasons which the doctor might give for stopping smoking.
   - Five arguments of the smoker against what the doctor says.
   
   The first ones are done for you.

Label each argument 'F' if it is a fact, rather than an opinion. Mark the facts '+' or '−' to show whether or not you support smoking.

2. After your class discussion, write down whose argument you thought was the most convincing, and why.

_____

_____

© Folens (copiable page)    ACTIVITY BANK: *Smoking*    9

Activity 4 – Teacher's notes

# Thinking ahead

*Recognising that young people may regard long-term health risks as unimportant*

## AIMS

To allow pupils to consider the risks of dismissing the long-term consequences of smoking.

### Teaching Points

*Materials needed*
Dice and counters for the board game.

- Young people who decide to start smoking take considerable risks with their future health.
- The tar in tobacco can cause many kinds of cancer such as cancer of the mouth, tongue, throat, lungs, pancreas, kidney, bladder and cervix.
- Chemicals from tobacco may damage the lining of the blood vessels. This causes a reduction of the oxygen supply to the heart and may lead to angina. It may also cause clots to form in the blood which may lead to a heart attack.
- Tobacco is the only legally-available consumer product that kills people when it is used entirely as intended.
- Because tobacco is addictive, young people who choose to start smoking are making a decision that they may find difficult to change in later life.
- For young people, later adult years can seem so far ahead as to be unimportant. Long-term risks are often perceived as less significant than immediate consequences.
- Presenting pupils with the ways in which smokers deal with long-term risks encourages them to acknowledge such risks in their own decision making.

## USING THE ACTIVITY SHEET

The focus of the activity is to consider the long-term effects of smoking by looking at the facts.

**Step 1** Hand out copies of Smoking Fact Sheet 2. Discuss with the class some of the reasons why they think young people take up smoking.

**Step 2** Split the class into small groups and hand out copies of the activity sheet to each group. Using counters and a dice, pupils play the board game (note that many of the pupils won't finish the game).

**Step 3** Discuss with the class whether they think many people consider the health risks when they start smoking. Why do some people continue to smoke in spite of the risks?

**Step 4** In their groups, ask the pupils to answer the last part of the activity sheet. Invite them to feed back their answers in a class discussion.

### Extension Activities

- Ask the pupils to carry out a survey of at least three adult smokers, asking them at what age they started, whether they considered the health risks and how they feel about it now.
- Ask pupils to design a poster warning young people against the long-term health risks of smoking.

### Outcomes

- A greater awareness of the way in which young people often discount long-term health risks.
- An increased likelihood that such risks will be considered when making a decision.
- Further development of skills of evaluation through assessing long-term health risks.

**Activity Sheet 4**

# Thinking ahead

1. In your groups, play the Smoking Risks board game.

| | | | | | |
|---|---|---|---|---|---|
| **START** <br> 1 | 2 | Out of breath – go back to START <br> 3 | 4 | 5 | Smoker's cough – go back 2 spaces <br> 6 |
| 12 | High blood pressure – go back to START <br> 11 | 10 | Out of breath – go back 3 spaces <br> 9 | 8 | 7 |
| Cancer of throat – go back to START <br> 13 | 14 | High blood pressure – go back 10 spaces <br> 15 | 16 | Angina – go back 10 spaces <br> 17 | 18 |
| 24 | Stroke – go back to START <br> 23 | 22 | 21 | Smoker's cough – go back 2 spaces <br> 20 | Cancer of pancreas – out of game <br> 19 |
| 25 | Chronic bronchitis – go back 10 spaces <br> 26 | 27 | Angina – go back 10 spaces <br> 28 | 29 | 30 |
| **FINISH** <br> 36 | 35 | Emphysema – go back 15 spaces <br> 34 | 33 | Heart attack – out of game <br> 32 | Lung cancer – out of game <br> 31 |

2. On the back of the sheet, write down one sentence of advice that you would give to a younger person who has just started smoking.

© Folens (copiable page)   ACTIVITY BANK: *Smoking*

**Activity 5 – Teacher's notes**

# Counting the cost

*Calculating the financial costs of smoking*

## AIMS

To make young people aware that smoking can be an extremely expensive habit in financial terms.

### Teaching Points

- An average packet of 20 cigarettes may not seem too expensive, but over a period of months or years the cost can really build up.
- Taxation accounts for 80% of the cost of cigarettes. In recent years, the Government has used taxation to raise the price of cigarettes in order to deter people from smoking.
- Although cigarette consumption tends to fall as the price rises, many smokers in low-income households are unwilling or unable to quit. Increasing taxation therefore means that they spend an even greater proportion of their income on cigarettes. This can be particularly problematic in low-income households, because of its effect on the family's budget.
- Children are among the groups most influenced by price. Because their incomes are often very limited, an increase in cigarette prices can put smoking increasingly out of their reach.

## USING THE ACTIVITY SHEET

The focus of the activity is for pupils to calculate for themselves the financial cost of smoking and consider its effect on their lifestyles.

**Step 1** Hand out copies of Smoking Fact Sheet 1 and ensure that the pupils know the current price of a packet of cigarettes. They should complete the first two questions on the sheet.

**Step 2** Invite the pupils to share their answers with the class. Are they surprised at the cost of smoking?

**Step 3** Ask the pupils to plan a short story about someone who has decided to give up smoking. They should follow the prompts on the activity sheet.

**Step 4** Discuss the pupils' story plans and encourage them to suggest helpful titles for one another's stories that highlight what the protagonist gains by giving up smoking (e.g. 'man swaps cigs for sports car!')

### Extension Activities

- The pupils could write a short story based on their story plans in a form that would be effective for a younger audience.
- The class can hold a mock House of Commons debate to decide what to do about tobacco tax. One pupil can take the part of the Chancellor of the Exchequer proposing to increase the tax on cigarettes. Other pupils can be MPs arguing for or against this proposal.

### Outcomes

- A knowledge of the long-term costs of smoking.
- Analysing the impact this has on a person's lifestyle.

**Activity Sheet 5**

# Counting the cost

The average price of a packet of cigarettes is [        ]

1. If a person smokes 20 cigarettes a day, how much is spent on smoking:

   in one week? [        ]   in one year? [        ]   in ten years? [        ]

2. Write shopping lists of the things you would like to buy for yourself with the money spent by the smokers in (a) one week and (b) one year.

   **Shopping list (a)**

   **Shopping list (b)**

3. On the back of the sheet, plan a short story about someone who has decided to give up smoking. You could include:

   a. The reasons they became a smoker.

   b. The reasons they decided to give up.

   c. Other people who may have been involved in the decision.

   d. How they felt about their new lifestyle.

**Activity 6 – Teacher's notes**

# An irritating habit

*Introducing the phenomenon of passive smoking*

## AIMS

To inform pupils that smoking can be an anti-social habit that causes distress and annoyance to non-smokers.

### Teaching Points

- Passive smoking involves involuntarily breathing in other people's smoke, either from the burning tip of a cigarette or from the smoke that has been inhaled and then exhaled by the smoker.
- Although 'no smoking' areas are increasingly common in public places and on public transport, non-smokers might still be subjected to other people's tobacco smoke: at home and in public places.
- Tobacco smoke can be very unpleasant to non-smokers. Effects can include sore eyes, coughs, sore throats, headaches, nausea, dizziness and the smell of stale tobacco on clothes and hair.
- The effects can be distressing for people who are ill or have breathing difficulties. Passive smoking can increase the severity of asthma attacks.
- Passive smoking can also cause other cancers and serious chest diseases (e.g. chronic bronchitis and emphysema).
- Most people who die from lung cancer are smokers. But when a non-smoker develops this disease, passive smoking is frequently responsible.

## USING THE ACTIVITY SHEET

**The focus of the activity is to explore the extent to which tobacco smoke can affect other people and a smoker's surroundings.**

**Step 1** Brainstorm with the whole class the concept of passive smoking, where it may occur and some of the effects. Hand out copies of Smoking Fact Sheet 3. Ask pupils to think about their own experiences of passive smoking and to write about their feelings in the first question on the activity sheet.

**Step 2** Invite pupils, in pairs, to think of other groups who suffer particularly from passive smoking and complete the second question on the activity sheet.

**Step 3** In small groups, ask the class to think about some of the effects on the smoker's surroundings caused by smoking and ask pupils to record them on the activity sheet.

**Step 4** Finally, hold a class discussion on what pupils have learned about passive smoking and ask them to complete the final question on the activity sheet.

### Extension Activities

- Ask pupils to compose a set of rules that smokers should follow to be considerate to others. They can then present this to the rest of the class.
- Ask the pupils to interview a smoker and a non-smoker about passive smoking. Their results can be combined as a survey and displayed for others in the school to read.

### Outcomes

- Understanding why people who inflict their tobacco smoke on others are unpopular.
- Recognising that smoking can be an anti-social, rather than a socially-desirable habit.
- Assessing the health and environmental implications of passive smoking.

**Activity Sheet 6**

# An irritating habit

Most people in Britain today are non-smokers. But non-smokers often find that they have to breathe in other people's tobacco smoke. This is called passive smoking.

1. Think about some occasions when you have been a passive smoker. Write them in the smoke clouds.

What effects did it have on you?

_____

How do you feel about this?

_____

2. Which people in particular might be harmed by passive smoking?

_____

3. What do you think the effects of smoking might be on the smoker's surroundings?

_____
_____

4. Write down what you have learned about passive smoking. Which effects of passive smoking were the most surprising and why?

_____
_____

© Folens (copiable page)     ACTIVITY BANK: *Smoking*

Activity 7 – Teacher's notes

# A smoker in the family

*Why parents need to protect their children from passive smoking in the home*

## AIMS

To inform pupils that their decision on whether or not to smoke may have implications for their own children's health.

## Teaching Points

*Materials needed*
Card or paper, coloured pens or pencils.
Leaflets on other health-related topics (these should be available from your local Health Promotion Department).

- The likelihood of stillbirth and miscarriage is increased when the mother smokes.
- Babies born to mothers who smoke tend to weigh less.
- Children of parents who smoke: suffer more frequent coughs and chest problems; are more likely to develop asthma; develop more ear, nose and throat problems; are more likely to have to be admitted to a hospital with chest problems; are more likely to develop serious chest diseases or cancer when they are older.
- Smoking by the mother is a major cause of 'cot death' (Sudden Infant Death Syndrome).
- It should be stressed that, because tobacco is addictive, some parents may find it very hard to stop smoking and care should be taken to avoid appearing to blame parents who smoke.
- Emphasis should be placed upon the need for pupils to consider the implications for their own future families when deciding whether or not to start smoking.

## USING THE ACTIVITY SHEET

**The focus of the activity is to consider how passive smoking can affect the health of others in the family.**

**Step 1** Hand out copies of Smoking Fact Sheet 3 and make available any leaflets that may stimulate the activity. Split the class into groups, handing a copy of the activity sheet to each. Allocate one statement to each group.

**Step 2** Ask each group to present their arguments to the rest of the class. Hold a class vote before and after each presentation – either for or against the statements.

**Step 3** In the same groups, ask the pupils to work on the second part of the activity sheet.

**Step 4** To consolidate the activity, pupils could draw up leaflets in their groups and pass around the class for discussion.

## Extension Activities

- Ask the pupils, singly or in pairs, to compile lists of reasons for a parent to (i) stop smoking and (ii) carry on smoking (e.g. the mother might feel that it helps her to cope with stress). Collate responses and hold a class discussion to decide which list outweighs the other.
- Invite a local midwife to visit the class to explain more of the facts about smoking in pregnancy. Discuss why so many pregnant women ignore their midwives' advice about smoking.

## Outcomes

- An understanding of the effects of parental smoking on children's health.
- Assessing possible implications for one's own future family when deciding whether or not to start smoking.
- Developing presentation and design skills.

# A smoker in the family

1. In your groups, discuss one of the following statements:

    - A pregnant woman shouldn't take any risks with her baby's health.
    - A pregnant woman has the right to smoke if she wants to.
    - A girl shouldn't start smoking if she wants to have children some day.
    - If a pregnant woman has a male partner, he should stop smoking too.

    After your discussion, write down two arguments from your group, both for and against the statement.

    | For | Against |
    |-----|---------|
    |     |         |
    |     |         |
    |     |         |
    |     |         |

    Now present your results to the rest of the class.

2. Design an information leaflet for parents who are smokers.

    Which facts do you want to include about how passive smoking can affect other people in the family?

    Use this sheet to write down your ideas.

    _____
    _____
    _____
    _____

    Decide what kind of approach you want to take. Do you want your leaflet to be 'hard-hitting' or more 'light-hearted'? Which approach do you think will have most effect?

    Write your reasons below.

    _____
    _____
    _____

**Activity 8 – Teacher's notes**

# No smoking!

*Considering the case for smoke-free areas*

## AIMS

To raise awareness of cases for and against smoking restrictions in different settings.

### Teaching Points

- Recent years have seen a considerable increase in the number of settings in which smoking is restricted or banned altogether.
- Now that smokers are in the minority in the UK, non-smokers are increasingly unwilling to tolerate the unpleasant and harmful effects of passive smoking.
- A number of workers have received compensation from their employers because other people's smoking in the workplace has caused illness. As a result, more and more companies are refusing to allow smoking at work or restricting it to a few separate areas.
- There are other benefits to be gained from banning smoking: fire risks are reduced (so insurance premiums may be cut) and there is less dirt on floors and walls (so cleaning and decorating bills are lower).
- Surveys have shown that even smokers frequently accept that smoking bans are a good idea. Many accept that it isn't fair to inflict their tobacco smoke on other people.

## USING THE ACTIVITY SHEET

**The focus of the activity is for pupils to consider and identify the places where they feel smoking should be restricted or banned.**

**Step 1**   Hand out copies of Smoking Fact Sheet 4. With the whole class, brainstorm some areas where pupils think smoking should be banned.

**Step 2**   Ask pupils to complete the activity sheet.

**Step 3**   Collate responses to question 2 in three columns on the board. On which areas are most pupils agreed? Where do they disagree?

**Step 4**   Hold a class debate on the particular issues raised by smoking in different sorts of places (e.g. where people have to work or receive education, travel, eat, spend their leisure time). It might be argued that a non-smoker can choose whether or not to go into a smoky pub, but does not have such a choice when it comes to their workplace.

### Extension Activities

- Ask the pupils to research the safety issues of passive smoking (e.g. smoke setting off fire alarms). Contact The Health and Safety Executive for an information leaflet (see Useful addresses page 47).
- Ask pupils to carry out a survey of smoking bans in their own community. In how many places is smoking still allowed? What sort of places are they? Why is smoking still allowed here? How could you set about trying to persuade one of the places where smoking is still allowed to introduce a ban?

### Outcomes

- An understanding of the different views of smokers and non-smokers on smoking bans.
- A greater awareness of some of the issues involved in making policy decisions in the community.

**Activity Sheet 8**

# No smoking!

1. For each of the places (including types of transport) shown in this town, indicate whether you think smoking should be banned, allowed or restricted to separate areas.

2. Make lists of those places where you think smoking should be banned, allowed or restricted. Give your reasons on the back of the sheet.

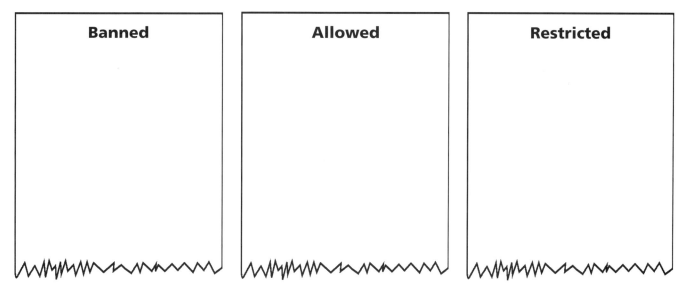

| Banned | Allowed | Restricted |
|---|---|---|
| | | |

© Folens (copiable page)     ACTIVITY BANK: *Smoking*

Activity 9 – Teacher's notes

# How many young people smoke?

*The facts about young smokers*

## AIMS

To examine the current statistics for young smokers and to consider the reasons for this.

### Teaching Points

- The tobacco industry has a particular problem in that it depends on a product that kills many of its customers. Each year, it needs to find new customers to replace those who have died or succeeded in stopping smoking.
- By the time they are 16, two-thirds of all young people have tried a cigarette[2].
- Now, among fifteen-year-olds, about one boy in four, and one girl in three, is a regular smoker.
- See Smoking Fact Sheet 1 for further statistics about young people and smoking.

## USING THE ACTIVITY SHEET

The focus of the activity is to consider the percentage of young people who smoke and whether smoking is more popular among girls or boys.

**Step 1** Discuss briefly with the class whether they think that most young people's decision to smoke is an independent one.

**Step 2** Hand out copies of the activity sheet and ask pupils, working individually or in pairs, to answer the first two questions. Invite them to share their answers with the whole class. Tabulate the results on the board.

**Step 3** Hand out copies of Smoking Fact Sheet 1. Invite pupils to compare the facts with their answers. Have any of them changed their opinion and why?

**Step 4** Ask the pupils to complete the final part of the activity sheet.

### Extension Activities

- Invite pupils to find out how the percentages of boys and girls in the UK who smoke have changed over the past twenty years. (Your local Health Promotion Department should be able to help with this.) They could tabulate their results using ICT skills.
- Invite pupils to research what tobacco companies are doing to avoid losing revenue. Do they conduct research into health issues?

### Outcomes

- An increased knowledge of the number of young people who smoke.
- Assessing the arguments for and against young people smoking and evaluating whether they have to smoke in order to be accepted by others.
- Developing presenting and collating skills.

**Activity Sheet 9**

# How many young people smoke?

1. Why does the tobacco industry always need to find new customers?

   _____
   _____
   _____


2. At what age do you think most young people start to smoke?

   _____

   Why might they start?

   _____
   _____
   _____

   Would many believe that they are likely to smoke as adults?

   _____

   Would many like to stop?

   _____

3. What did you find most surprising about the facts that you learned and why?

   _____
   _____
   _____
   _____
   _____
   _____
   _____

© Folens (copiable page)　　　ACTIVITY BANK: *Smoking*

**Activity 10 – Teacher's notes**

# Good for your image?

*Further implications of smoking for self-image*

## AIMS

To consider further why some young people may feel that smoking is good for their image and recognise how a positive self-image can be achieved without smoking.

## Teaching Points

- Most of us care what other people think about us. We are keen to have a good image.
- We do different things to try to give ourselves the image we want. For example, we may try to shape our image through the clothes we wear, the way we speak, what we eat and drink, the music we listen to, the places we're seen in and (when we are older) the car we drive.
- Some young people choose to smoke because they think smoking is good for their image. They may think it makes them look more attractive or cool.
- Young people may be more inclined to try smoking to bolster their image if they are less self-confident and happy with themselves.
- Young people should be encouraged to consider how smoking may have a negative effect on their image and how they can use other means to improve their image without turning to smoking.

## USING THE ACTIVITY SHEET

The focus of the activity is to consider how a young person of the pupils' own age can improve his or her own image.

**Step 1**  With the whole class, brainstorm some things that help to define a young person's image (e.g. clothes, hair, friends, activities). Ask the class what these things might say about a person's image. Write these on the board.

**Step 2**  Now ask the class for some words to describe what image smoking portrays. Write these on the board.

**Step 3**  Compare the two lists. Was the second list more positive or negative than the first? If pupils thought that smoking gave a positive image, can they suggest other ways to achieve this?

**Step 4**  Ask pupils to complete the activity sheet. Invite them to feed back some of their answers in a class discussion.

## Extension Activities

- Ask pupils to identify some famous smokers from television programmes. Ask pupils to consider how their image would be affected if they stopped smoking.
- Look for examples of smoking depicted in magazines read by young people. Hold a TV-style debate with a chairperson and 'guest' audience. Does the media glamorise smoking? Should they do this?

## Outcomes

- Evaluating further influences on the personal decision of whether or not to smoke.
- An awareness of ways of having a good image without smoking.

**Activity Sheet 10**

# Good for your image?

Write about an imaginary young person of your own age. Give the young person you are writing about a name. Write that name in the space below and then answer the questions.

Name _____

Good points _____
_____
_____

Not-so-good points _____
_____
_____

Are they happy with their image? _____
_____
_____

How could they improve their image? _____
_____
_____

Would smoking improve their image? _____
_____
_____

Could smoking make it worse? _____
_____
_____

What could they do to have a good image without smoking? ___
_____
_____
_____

**Activity 11 – Teacher's notes**

# Fooled by the ads

*How advertising tries to present a positive image of smoking*

## AIMS

To increase awareness of the ways in which tobacco companies have used advertising and sponsorship to try to make smoking appeal to people.

## Teaching Points

*Materials needed*
Advertisements from magazines, particularly those concerned with image.

- Tobacco companies have always spent heavily on advertising their products. Although TV advertising of cigarettes has been banned in the UK for a number of years, until recently there continued to be a great deal of advertising through magazines, newspapers and billboards.
- Tobacco companies have also made considerable use of indirect advertising, for example by sponsoring major sports events (e.g. Formula One racing) and brand stretching (applying the tobacco brand and logo to other products such as clothing).
- The tobacco industry has argued that advertising is aimed only at existing smokers, to promote brand loyalty and switching between brands, but there is strong evidence that advertising has encouraged young people to start smoking.
- Young people seem to have been particularly influenced by advertising and sports sponsorship and have tended to buy those brands that have been advertised most heavily[2].

## USING THE ACTIVITY SHEET

**The focus of the activity is to become aware of the effects that advertising has had on young people.**

**Step 1** With the class, look at how magazine, billboard and television advertising glamorises a product.

**Step 2** Split the class into groups and hand out copies of the activity sheet to each group. Ask the pupils to complete question 1 (remind them to think carefully about young people's thoughts and behaviour). Invite them to feed back their answers in a class discussion.

**Step 3** Hand out the copies of Smoking Fact Sheet 5. Ask the pupils to complete question 2. Each group should describe the different parts of the campaign and explain the reasons for these (e.g. is it planned to sponsor a particular sports event? Why?). Groups could also design adverts that might appear in magazines or billboards.

**Step 4** Ask each group to present its ideas.

**Step 5** Hold a class debate about these ideas and how they relate to real cigarette advertising. Encourage the class to consider how advertising has sought to influence young people. Does advertising always tell the truth? Does it try to mislead?

## Extension Activities

- Ask pupils to compare two cigarette advertising campaigns. What are the differences and similarities? How do they each try to influence behaviour?

## Outcomes

- Evaluating the effects of advertising on young people's thoughts and behaviour.
- Developing presentation and design skills.

**Activity Sheet 11**

# Fooled by the ads

1. How has cigarette advertising tried to influence young people in particular?

   _____
   _____

2. Work in a group.

   Imagine that you have been asked to plan an advertising campaign for a new brand of cigarettes. Think up your own brand name and write some ideas for a slogan. The campaign has to be aimed at young people.

   _____
   _____
   _____
   _____

3. Draw a design for a visual display.

© Folens (copiable page)     ACTIVITY BANK: *Smoking*

**Activity 12 – Teacher's notes**

# Should ads be banned?

*The case for banning tobacco advertising*

## AIMS

To describe current and planned restrictions on tobacco advertising and the justification for these.

### Teaching Points

- Although direct TV advertising of cigarettes is banned in the UK, the Government has largely relied on voluntary agreements with the tobacco industry to restrict the impact of advertising on young people.
- In addition to ending all billboard advertising, the Government is now committed to implementing a new EU Directive that will end tobacco sponsorship by July 2003 (2006 in special cases).
- The ban on sponsorship has led many sports to claim they have had difficulty in finding funds to replace it.
- The Directive still allows advertising in specialist tobacconist shops, under strict control.

## USING THE ACTIVITY SHEET

**The focus of the activity is to increase awareness of the debate on whether or not to ban different types of tobacco advertising.**

**Step 1** Brainstorm some reasons 'for' and 'against' tobacco advertising and write them in two columns on the board.

**Step 2** Ask the class to complete the first part of the activity sheet.

**Step 3** Provide pupils with background information on the composition and procedures of the House of Commons. Set up a mock Chamber, with Government and Opposition benches and a Speaker's chair. Identify volunteers to play the roles of Speaker and MPs to speak in the debate for and against advertising bans.

**Step 4** Provide pupils with copies of Smoking Fact Sheet 5. Give the MPs time to prepare their speeches. Make sure that speeches are brief and to the point, with reasons for taking a particular stance.

**Step 5** Hold votes to decide whether all tobacco advertising should be banned or some forms (such as sponsorship) should still be allowed.

**Step 6** Ask pupils to complete the second part of the activity sheet.

### Extension Activities

- Ask pupils to carry out a survey involving the school or local community to find out which cigarette companies are associated with which sports. Results could be presented in graphs and tables.
- Pupils could research recent changes in the cigarette advertising law using the Internet.

### Outcomes

- An understanding of the cases for and against advertising bans.
- A further evaluation of, and ability to resist, tobacco advertising.

**Activity Sheet 12**

# Should ads be banned?

1. As a class, you are going to hold your own House of Commons debate to decide whether the present law on cigarette advertising in Britain should be changed.

   Think of five arguments for all cigarette advertising being banned.

   Write them below.

   _____
   _____
   _____
   _____
   _____

   Now think of five arguments against all cigarette advertising being banned.

   Write them below. (The tobacco companies might argue that the law should stay as it is or they might propose that the present restrictions on advertising should be removed.)

   _____
   _____
   _____
   _____
   _____

   In your debate, consider whether tobacco companies should be allowed to continue to sponsor sports competitions or other public events.

2. After your class debate, which argument did you think was the most convincing and why?

   _____
   _____
   _____

**Activity 13 – Teacher's notes**

# Going along with the crowd

*The effects of peer pressure*

## AIMS

To increase pupils' awareness of the effects of peer pressure and improve their ability to resist this.

### Teaching Points

- Young people are more likely to become smokers if they have a brother or sister, or friends, who smoke.
- Peer pressure can operate in a number of different ways. Some young people tend to look to others for a lead, and easily imitate the behaviour of others around them.
- Some young people take up smoking because they feel this is necessary to be accepted into a particular group. They feel they will not be allowed to belong if they don't smoke like other group members.
- In some cases, young people can find themselves being pressurised into smoking even though they don't want to. They can succumb to constant nagging or ridicule.
- Not all young people give in to peer pressure. Some are leaders rather than followers, deciding behaviour for themselves and others. Some develop skills that allow them to resist peer pressure, such as using humour or making themselves valuable to the group in other ways.
- Young people are less likely to succumb to peer pressure if they are enabled to recognise its influence and to develop and practise resistance skills.

## USING THE ACTIVITY SHEET

The focus of the activity to explore how peer pressure operates and to try out ways of resisting.

**Step 1** With the whole class, brainstorm some words to describe peer pressure.

**Step 2** Ask for volunteers to act out a scene in which a non-smoker wants to join a group of young friends who all smoke. The scene can be repeated with new groups of volunteers as many times as required.

**Step 3** The rest of the class can offer suggestions on what the smokers might say and how the non-smoker might respond. The audience could be allowed to stop and 'rewind' the action at appropriate points.

**Step 4** Encourage the class to identify different ways in which peer pressure can operate and alternative methods of resisting or deflecting it.

**Step 5** Divide the class into pairs. One of the pair is the young person exerting the pressure to smoke, the other has to resist this pressure. The roles are reversed after a few minutes. This allows all pupils to practise resistance skills.

**Step 6** Ask pupils to complete the activity sheet.

### Extension Activities

- Hold a class discussion of the issues raised by the activity. How reasonable is it to exert pressure on others? How can peer pressure be discouraged?
- Ask pupils to design posters to discourage young people from exerting pressure on others and offering tips on how to resist pressure.

### Outcomes

- A greater awareness of how peer pressure can operate.
- Assertiveness in being able to resist peer pressure.

**Activity Sheet 13**

# Going along with the crowd

Imagine that you are an agony aunt or uncle and you have been sent these letters. Write a reply with suggestions of what they should do.

Dear Sam
My best friend has joined a new group of friends to go out with. They are a really popular group but they all smoke. My friend says I should join in but I don't like smoking. What can I do? Please help!
Cara

**Dear Cara**

Dear Sam
I am worried about losing my friends. They have started smoking in the lunch break. I don't like the smell of smoke so I can't go along with them but I have no one else to talk to. I don't want to lose their friendship but they are beginning to leave me out of their plans. What can I do?
Please help!
Greg

**Dear Greg**

**Activity 14 – Teacher's notes**

# Hooked on tobacco

*How taking up smoking can mean losing control*

## AIMS

To increase awareness that when young people start smoking they can find it difficult or impossible to stop.

### Teaching Points

- Tobacco smoke contains nicotine. Nicotine is a powerful drug that acts on the brain and can cause addiction.
- When a smoker inhales, nicotine passes from the lungs into the blood vessels. It reaches the brain within seconds.
- Smokers who go without cigarettes often suffer nicotine withdrawal symptoms. These include feeling depressed, feeling anxious, being irritable and bad-tempered, finding it hard to concentrate, losing sleep and putting on weight.
- Cigarette smoking can become a habit too. Smokers become used to having a cigarette in certain situations, but addiction is the main reason most smokers find it hard to stop.
- Young smokers often believe that they will stop smoking before they become addicted and will be able to stay in control.
- In fact, addiction can happen very quickly. Before they realise it, young people can find themselves hooked on tobacco.

## USING THE ACTIVITY SHEET

**The focus of the activity is to consider the effects of nicotine withdrawal on a smoker for one day.**

**Step 1** Ask the class to research symptoms of nicotine withdrawal using the Internet and CD-ROM facilities. Discuss their findings and list these symptoms on the board. Hand out copies of Smoking Fact Sheet 4 and add any new facts to the list.

**Step 2** Give out copies of the activity sheet and ask pupils to write out, individually, a simple story-line and create their own cartoon strip.

**Step 3** Display the completed strips for the class to view.

**Step 4** Hold a class discussion on the addictive nature of cigarettes and the problems of losing control to tobacco.

### Extension Activities

- Ask the class to carry out a survey of pupils in the school to find out how easy they think it is for a young person to stop smoking when they choose to.
- Invite a young adult who is now hooked on tobacco to talk to the class about their experience.

### Outcomes

- A recognition of the addictive nature of tobacco.
- An understanding that the best way of staying in control is not to start smoking.

**Activity Sheet 14**

# Hooked on tobacco

Working alone, create a cartoon strip that tells the story of a smoker having to go all day without cigarettes. You could call it 'Dying For A Cigarette' or else think up a title yourself.

You need to come up with a story-line that has a clear beginning, a middle and an end. You might want to include something about:
- the times when the smoker really misses a cigarette
- the withdrawal symptoms the smoker suffers
- the effects on other people.

© Folens (copiable page)      ACTIVITY BANK: *Smoking*

**Activity 15 – Teacher's notes**

# Breaking the habit

*The smokers who want to stop*

## AIMS

To show that many smokers want to stop smoking but find it difficult to do so.

### Teaching Points

- Surveys show that two-thirds of smokers say they would like to stop. This applies to young smokers as well as to people who have been smoking for many years.
- Many smokers do manage to beat their addiction to tobacco, but they are likely to have tried and failed a few times before finally succeeding.
- Smokers may decide they want to stop because of worries about their health or appearance, financial cost, pressure from family or recognition that most people disapprove of smoking.
- Reasons for failing to give up smoking may include not being sufficiently mentally prepared, being irritable with family or others, finding stress hard to cope with, feeling tired and depressed and increased appetite or putting on weight.
- Young people who are thinking of, or have just started, smoking need to be aware that many smokers do not want to carry on smoking and that stopping can be difficult, but that initial failure to stop does not rule out ultimate success.

## USING THE ACTIVITY SHEET

The focus of the activity is to examine some of the reasons why smokers find it difficult to stop smoking and to think of possible solutions to these difficulties.

**Step 1** Discuss with the whole class whether they know anyone who is trying to give up smoking. Ask them to complete question 1 of the activity sheet. Hand out copies of Smoking Fact Sheet 4. Compare the facts to your class discussions.

**Step 2** In pairs, ask pupils to take on the role of a smoker who is trying to give up and a friend who is trying to help them. The smoker must explain their difficulties and the friend must try to offer solutions. Ask them to swap roles. Then complete questions 2 and 3 of the activity sheet.

**Step 3** Divide the board into two columns headed 'difficulties' and 'solutions'. Invite the class to feed back their answers to question 3.

### Extension Activities

- Ask pupils to research national survey data on percentages of people who (a) want to stop and (b) have stopped smoking (they could use the Internet). Ask pupils to apply these percentages to work out numbers in these categories in their own community.
- Ask pupils to write a newspaper article telling the story of one smoker's struggle to break free from cigarettes.

### Outcomes

- An understanding of and empathy with the difficulties smokers face in stopping smoking.
- An understanding that it is best never to start smoking or to stop before the habit becomes too established.

**Activity Sheet 15**

# Breaking the habit

1. Do you think most smokers would like to stop smoking? Give reasons for your answer.

   _____
   _____

2. List five reasons why smokers might want to stop smoking.

   _____
   _____
   _____
   _____
   _____

   Now list five reasons why these attempts might fail.

   _____
   _____
   _____
   _____
   _____

3. Do you think it is possible to stop the smoking habit? What advice would you give a smoker who is trying to stop?

   _____
   _____
   _____
   _____
   _____
   _____
   _____
   _____

**Activity 16 – Teacher's notes**

# Who needs cigarettes?

*Why some people may think they need to keep smoking*

## AIMS

To identify other ways of achieving the perceived benefits of cigarettes without smoking.

## Teaching Points

- Many young people may feel they need to smoke in order to cope with the stress in their lives.
- Young people can face stress from many sources, and it is important that they develop techniques for coping with stress and relaxing.
- Smokers may come to depend on cigarettes instead of learning better ways of coping and unwinding.
- Some young people (particularly girls) also see cigarettes as a way of controlling their weight. For many young people, being slim is an important priority and girls who smoke are often afraid to stop because they believe this will lead to weight gain.
- Smoking can suppress appetite and smokers who stop may eat more and so gain weight. But this effect can be controlled by choosing the right foods and taking more exercise.

## USING THE ACTIVITY SHEET

**The focus of the activity is to think of ways of handling stress and addressing the weight issue without relying on cigarettes.**

**Step 1** In this activity it is important to be particularly sensitive to the needs of individual pupils, some of whom may be self-conscious about their weight or currently experiencing high levels of stress.

**Step 2** Ask the class to suggest reasons why some young people feel they need cigarettes. Stress and weight are almost certain to be referred to spontaneously but, if not, ask the class if they think these may also be reasons. If other important reasons are suggested, adapt the activity to allow pupils to think of alternative ways of dealing with these factors without relying on cigarettes.

**Step 3** Divide the class into small groups, and provide each group with an activity sheet. Identify pupils to write the answers and report on these to the class.

**Step 4** When all groups have reported, ask the class to consider whether young people really need to rely on cigarettes.

## Extension Activities

- With the class, learn about relaxation techniques, such as yoga. Invite visitors to talk about and demonstrate these.
- With the class, learn about ways of using physical activity to reduce stress and control weight.

## Outcomes

- A greater awareness of alternative ways of coping with stress.
- A recognition that weight control is not a valid reason for smoking.
- The development of problem-solving skills.

**Activity Sheet 16**

# Who needs cigarettes?

On the arrows below, write some of the things that cause stress to young people.

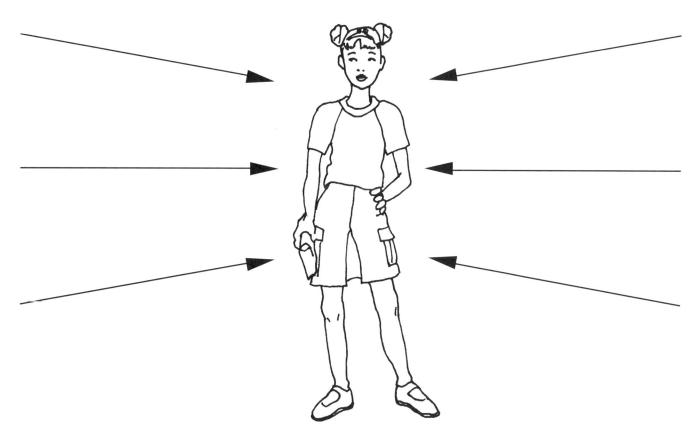

Now make up a list of up to ten things which young people can do to relax and unwind – without smoking cigarettes!

_____     _____
_____     _____
_____     _____
_____     _____
_____     _____

Report your lists to the class.

© Folens (copiable page)   ACTIVITY BANK: *Smoking*

**Activity 17 – Teacher's notes**

# How to quit

*Tried and tested ways to stop smoking*

## AIMS

To inform on methods which can be used to improve chances of success in stopping smoking.

## Teaching Points

*Materials needed*
Copies of leaflets that provide advice on how to stop smoking from your local Health Promotion Department or school nurse.

- Stopping smoking can be difficult and, for some people, impossible. But every day in Britain more than one thousand people stop smoking for good.
- There is no single method of stopping smoking that works for everyone. Different people find different approaches helpful.
- Smokers who are heavily addicted to nicotine can be helped by some form of nicotine replacement therapy, such as patches or gum, but this is not appropriate for all adult smokers, nor is it suitable for children.
- Some people claim to have been helped by alternative methods like hypnotherapy and acupuncture, but such methods have not been properly evaluated and are therefore unproven[28].
- Many smokers prefer to have the support of others who are trying to quit and find it helpful to join stop-smoking self-help groups or clinics.
- Many smokers manage to stop smoking on their own, relying on will-power and determination and using a variety of tricks and techniques that work for them personally.
- Because most young smokers say they want to stop, pupils should be aware of effective methods that they can use themselves or to help a friend.

## USING THE ACTIVITY SHEET

**The focus of the activity is to draw up a ten-point plan for breaking free from cigarettes.**

**Step 1** Give out copies of leaflets on how to stop smoking to the class and hand out copies of Smoking Fact Sheet 4.

**Step 2** Invite one or more ex-smokers to tell the class what methods they used to help them stop. Try to find someone who came up with an unusual technique – the odder the better!

**Step 3** Pupils work alone on the activity sheets to write their own ten-point plan on How to Stop Smoking. They should try to think of some variations on recommended techniques rather than simply repeat what they read in the leaflets and information provided. Encourage them to think of ideas that might particularly work with smokers they know (perhaps themselves).

**Step 4** Feed back ideas to the class and agree a class ten-point plan to write on the board.

## Extension Activities

- Plan a service in your school to help smokers who want to stop (staff and pupils). This might include training some staff and pupils as advice counsellors.

## Outcomes

- A better understanding of how someone can stop smoking.
- A recognition that many young smokers succeed in stopping.

**Activity Sheet 17**

# How to quit

Write your own ten-point plan on how to stop smoking. You should be able to think of at least ten practical tips which smokers can use if they really want to give up smoking.

---

**Ten steps to stopping smoking**

1.

2.

3.

4.

5.

6.

7.

8.

9.

10.

---

If you are a smoker who wants to stop, you can use your ten-point plan yourself.
If you have friends, or people in your family, who want to quit smoking, you can use the plan to help them.

Activity 18 – Teacher's notes

# Illegal sales

*The law on cigarette sales to children*

## AIMS

To increase awareness of the law on cigarette sales and the reasons for this.

### Teaching Points

- Although it is not against the law for children to smoke, it is illegal to sell cigarettes to anyone under the age of 16.
- Shopkeepers are required to display a sign stating the law on tobacco sales to under 16s and those who do sell illegally can be prosecuted and fined.
- Trading Standards Officers employed by Local Authorities are responsible for enforcing this law. In many places, Trading Standards Officers work with children to check on shopkeepers. These children are specially selected and trained to go into shops and ask to buy cigarettes.
- In recent years, the Government has demanded that Trading Standards Officers take tougher action against shopkeepers breaking the law. It is argued that children are much more likely to become regular smokers if they find it easy to buy cigarettes.
- Others argue that catching out shopkeepers will not stop children getting hold of cigarettes in other ways.
- The UK Government makes around £100 million from illegal tobacco sales sold to children under 16[22].

## USING THE ACTIVITY SHEET

The focus of this activity is to consider, through group discussion, some key questions on the issue of sales to under 16s.

**Step 1** Find out what pupils know about the law on cigarette sales to children. Hand out Smoking Fact Sheet 5 and explain how Trading Standards Officers work with children to detect shopkeepers who break the law.

**Step 2** Hand out a copy of the activity sheet to each group. Split the class into discussion groups. Ask each group to appoint a chairperson to control the discussion and decide who will record and report the group's views on each question.

**Step 3** Representatives of the groups report back to the whole class on each question in turn. What are the views of the class as a whole? Is there more agreement on some questions than others? Results could be collated on the board.

### Extension Activities

- Invite a Trading Standards Officer to speak to the class about local law enforcement.
- Ask the pupils to devise a campaign to explain to shopkeepers why they shouldn't sell cigarettes to children.

### Outcomes

- An understanding of the law on cigarette sales and how it is enforced.
- Evaluating the morality of enabling children to smoke.

**Activity Sheet 18**

# Illegal sales

Write the answers to the following questions:

1. Will it stop children smoking if they cannot buy cigarettes?

   _____
   _____
   _____
   _____

2. What about other things that cannot be sold to children (e.g. lottery tickets and alcohol)? Should children be allowed to buy anything, or should there be more things they are not allowed to buy?

   _____
   _____
   _____
   _____
   _____

3. Should it be illegal to sell cigarettes to children?

   _____
   _____
   _____
   _____

4. How do you feel about children helping to catch shopkeepers who sell cigarettes illegally?

   _____
   _____
   _____
   _____

Activity 19 – Teacher's notes

# Making up your own mind

*Weighing the pros and cons of smoking*

## AIMS

To enable pupils to consider the costs and benefits of smoking and make their own informed decision.

### Teaching Points

- Most people decide whether or not to become a smoker at a relatively young age. This may be one of the most important decisions a person ever makes: it can determine future health and life-span, it can have serious financial consequences, and it can affect the health and comfort of others.
- Young people have to make up their own minds whether to smoke or not. It is vital that they are given the knowledge, ability and opportunity to make intelligent, considered decisions.
- A major concern is that, whereas young people can perceive the benefits of smoking as immediate, the main disadvantages can appear so long-term as to be of little consequence. Pupils should be encouraged to recognise the short-term disadvantages of smoking and to think long-term too.
- In this activity, the decision that pupils make is a personal one. They should not be required to announce or explain it. Provision should be made, however, for pupils who want to talk about smoking on a one-to-one basis or to obtain help with stopping.

## USING THE ACTIVITY SHEET

The focus of the activity is to consider the pros and cons of smoking, and weight these according to their own preferences to decide where the balance lies.

**Step 1** Ask the class to brainstorm the various pros and cons of smoking. (Copies of Smoking Fact Sheets 1 and 2 may be useful reminders.) List these on the board. Encourage the class to think of short- and long-term effects as well as important and less-important consequences.

**Step 2** Make it clear to pupils that they will not be expected to show anyone else what they have written on the activity sheet.

**Step 3** Pupils work on their own to complete the activity sheet, listing those pros and cons that apply to themselves and weighting them according to their relative importance to themselves.

**Step 4** Remind pupils what arrangements are available for them to obtain personal help and advice on smoking.

### Extension Activities

- Invite pupils to put together a plan to achieve the Government's targets to reduce smoking among 11- to 15-year-olds (to 11% by 2005 and 9% by 2010) in your school.
- Ask pupils to devise a programme to create a totally smoke-free environment in their local town. They could present their work using ICT skills.

### Outcomes

- Evaluating the range of factors that are important to young people regarding smoking.
- Giving pupils the opportunity to make a considered choice.

**Activity Sheet 19**

# Making up your own mind

Work on your own.

What does smoking mean to you?

- Cost?
- Image?
- Illness?
- Pleasure?
- Pollution?
- Popularity?

Make lists of all the good things and the bad things about smoking. Only include those things that you feel apply to you.

| Good things | Bad things |
|---|---|
|  |  |

Now consider how important each of these things is to you. Give each one a weight – in other words, put one of these numbers alongside it:

|  | **'weight'** |
|---|---|
| very important | 3 |
| fairly important | 2 |
| slightly important | 1 |
| not at all important | 0 |

Think carefully each time. Are things that might happen years from now less important than things that might happen straight away?

When you have given each item a number, add up the total 'weight' of each list. Which side is heaviest?

What is your decision about smoking?

_____

_____

_____

**Smoking Fact Sheet 1**

### The contents of cigarettes

- Tobacco smoke contains thousands of chemicals. Many of these chemicals are harmful to the human body.
- Some of the chemicals cause damage to the inner lining of blood vessels, causing them to become furred up.
- Irritants in tobacco smoke destroy the tiny hairs in the air passages that normally trap dirt and germs. As a result, dirt and germs are able to travel into the lungs and accumulate there.
- Tar is a black, sticky substance that collects in the lungs. It contains products that are known to cause cancer. Even so-called 'low-tar' cigarettes are dangerous.
- Smoking destroys the airsacs in the lung that are essential for supplying oxygen to the lung.
- Carbon monoxide is a poisonous gas that reduces the blood's ability to transport oxygen around the body. When someone smokes, the carbon monoxide in the smoke passes from the lungs into the blood vessels. Oxygen is needed to build cells and convert food into energy. Heavy smokers may have the oxygen-carrying power of their blood cut by as much as 15%[2].
- Nicotine is a powerful drug that affects the brain (making it addictive) and heart (putting a strain on it by increasing the heart beat rate and raising the blood pressure so that the heart needs more oxygen). In large quantities, nicotine is extremely poisonous.

### Counting the cost

- In 1999 a 20-a-day smoker will spend over £1200 on cigarettes[2].
- The price of tobacco is accepted by the tobacco and health industries to be the single greatest short-term influence on sales of cigarettes. Increasing levels of tax on cigarettes reduces the number of people who smoke[2].
- The Health Education Authority estimates that the cost to the NHS of treating diseases caused by smoking is £1.7 billion a year[8].
- In 1997, the Government earned £1915 million in VAT on tobacco[9] and spent only £7.5 million on anti-smoking campaigns[10].
- The number of smokers who take days off sick from work is greater than non-smokers, causing losses to their industry.

### Smoking and young people

- In the UK, about 450 children start smoking every day[16].
- Since the mid-1990s, smoking has been on the increase among 11- to 16-year-olds[2].
- The proportion of regular smokers increases sharply with age. A 1996 survey showed that 3% of 12-year-olds smoked regularly. This rose to 30% in 15-year-olds[19].
- 75% of regular smokers between 11 and 15 say they would find it hard to give up the habit[19].
- Among 15-year-olds, about one boy in four, and one girl in three, is a regular smoker.
- By the time they are 16, two-thirds of all young people have tried a cigarette.
- Half of all teenagers who currently smoke will die from diseases caused by tobacco if they continue to smoke. A quarter of them will die before the age of 70, losing, on average, 23 years of life[7].

**Smoking Fact Sheet 2**

**The short-term and visible effects of smoking**

- Cancer and heart disease may take years to develop in a smoker, but other harmful effects can show up relatively quickly when a young person starts to smoke.
- Smokers soon become more prone to coughs and chest infections. In comparison with non-smokers, they may have more days when they feel unwell and may not enjoy life to the full.
- Because tobacco reduces the body's ability to deliver the oxygen that fuels muscles, young smokers become less fit and find that they get out of breath more quickly.
- The chemicals in cigarette smoke also cause some unpleasant odours, affecting clothes and breath.
- Smoking harms the skin. It restricts the flow of blood to skin layers, causing them to wrinkle and age more quickly.
- Prolonged smoking causes the yellowing of fingers, fingernails and teeth.

**The long-term effects of smoking**

- The tar in tobacco smoke can cause many kinds of cancer. Inhaling tobacco smoke can lead to cancer of the mouth, tongue, throat, lungs, pancreas, kidney, bladder and, in women, cervix.
- Chemicals from tobacco smoke may damage the lining of the blood vessels. This slows down the supply of oxygen to the heart and causes angina (severe chest pain).
- Smoking accelerates the natural ageing process of the blood vessels, damaging their smooth inner lining. The blood carried inside this is then more likely to form clots. If a blood clot forms in one of the arteries supplying the heart and blocks the blood supply to the brain or heart, this can cause a heart attack or a stroke.
- The amount of oxygen carried in the blood is reduced by the carbon monoxide in tobacco smoke. The smoker's heart has to work harder. This may also lead to a heart attack.
- Tobacco is the only legally available consumer product that kills people when it is used entirely as intended.
- Smoking causes 120 000 deaths a year in the UK[4].
- About half of all regular cigarette smokers will eventually be killed by their habit[6].
- Smoking is the main cause of chronic lung disease. It is very rare in non-smokers and at least 80% of deaths related to it can be attributed to smoking[4].
- The younger the person is when he or she starts smoking, the greater the risk of developing lung cancer[2].
- In 1995 there were 46 000 cancer deaths in the UK attributed to smoking: approximately a third of all cancer deaths[4].
- Every year, tobacco smoking accounts for around 30 000 deaths from coronary heart disease in the UK or nearly 20% of all heart disease deaths[4].
- Pneumonia is more common amongst smokers and is more likely to be fatal. In 1995, 9900 deaths from pneumonia were attributed to smoking[4].

# Smoking Fact Sheet 3

## Passive smoking

- Passive smoking involves involuntarily breathing in other people's smoke, either from the burning tip of a cigarette or from the smoke that has been inhaled and then exhaled by the smoker.
- Passive smoking can increase the severity of asthma attacks.
- Passive smoking can cause other cancers and serious chest diseases (e.g. chronic bronchitis and emphysema).
- It is estimated that in the UK as many as 12 000 cases of heart disease each year can be attributed to passive smoking[16].
- Tobacco smoke can be very unpleasant to non-smokers. Effects can include sore eyes, coughs, sore throats, headaches, nausea, dizziness and the smell of stale tobacco on clothes and hair.
- The effects can be distressing for people who are already ill or have breathing difficulties.
- Most people who die from lung cancer are smokers. But when a non-smoker develops this disease, passive smoking is frequently responsible.
- Every day in Britain, one person dies from lung cancer caused by passive smoking.
- The risk of lung cancer in non-smokers exposed to passive smoking is increased by between 20% and 30%[5].
- Non-smokers are at an increased risk of heart attacks[11].

## Passive smoking in the home

- Children of parents who smoke:
  - are more likely to develop chest illnesses and coughs
  - are more likely to develop asthma
  - develop more ear, nose and throat problems
  - are more likely to have to be admitted to hospital with chest problems
  - are more likely to develop serious chest diseases or cancer when they are older[2].
- The likelihood of miscarriage is much higher in women who smoke[12].
- Passive smoking in the home may be the equivalent to a child smoking 80 cigarettes a year[21].
- Babies born to women who smoke are on average 200 grams (8oz) lighter than babies born to non-smoking mothers[2].
- Smoking by the mother is responsible for at least 25% of 'cot deaths' (Sudden Infant Death Syndrome)[16].
- The likelihood of a stillbirth is increased by about a third in smoking mothers[2].
- More than 17 000 children under five are admitted to hospital every year because of the effects of passive smoking[12].
- A recent survey shows that, in households where both parents smoke, young children have a 72% increased risk of respiratory illnesses[13].
- Each year in the UK, about 600 lung cancer deaths and up to 12 000 cases of heart disease in non-smokers can be attributed to passive smoking[14].

## Smoking Fact Sheet 4

### Considering smoke-free areas

- Recent years have seen an increase in the number of places where smoking is restricted or banned altogether (e.g. public transport and many places of work).
- A number of workers have received compensation from their employers because other people's smoking in the workplace has caused them illness. As a result, more and more companies are refusing to allow smoking at work or restricting it to a few separate areas.
- There are other benefits to be gained from banning smoking: fire risks are reduced (so insurance premiums may be cut) and there is less dirt on floors and walls (so cleaning and decorating bills are lower).
- A survey shows that 73% of the general public approved of a ban on smoking at work and 40% strongly approved of bans in all public places[15].
- A recent survey of street litter found that cigarette ends account for about 40% of street litter in the UK[17].
- Cigarettes and matches are a common cause of fires. In 1987, smoking materials were the most common cause of fire deaths[18].

### Tobacco addiction

- Tobacco smoke contains nicotine. Nicotine is a powerful drug that acts on the brain and can cause addiction.
- When a smoker inhales, nicotine passes from the lungs into the blood vessels. It reaches the brain within seconds.
- Smokers who go without cigarettes often suffer nicotine withdrawal symptoms. These include feeling depressed, feeling anxious, being irritable and bad-tempered, finding it hard to concentrate, losing sleep and putting on weight.
- Smoking can be addictive. Smokers become used to having a cigarette in certain situations. For this reason they find it hard to stop.
- It has been said that the way in which nicotine causes addiction is similar to drugs such as heroin and cocaine[3].

### Breaking the habit

- Many smokers do manage to beat their addiction to tobacco, but they are likely to have tried and failed a few times before finally succeeding.
- Smokers may decide they want to stop because of worries about their health or appearance, financial cost, pressure from family or recognition that most people disapprove of smoking.
- Reasons for failing to give up smoking may include not being sufficiently mentally prepared, being irritable with family or others, finding stress hard to cope with, feeling tired and depressed, and increased appetite or putting on weight.
- Long-term weight gain is only about 6–8lbs for each smoker who quits[26]. This is without attempts to diet or exercise.
- 70% of adults would like to give up according to a survey in 1998[5].
- Smokers who are heavily addicted to nicotine can be helped by some form of nicotine replacement therapy, such as patches or gum, but this is not suitable for all adult smokers or any children.
- Alternative methods of giving up smoking include hypnotherapy and acupuncture but these methods have not been properly evaluated or proven[1].
- Herbal cigarettes are not recommended because they produce both tar and carbon monoxide and reinforce the habit of smoking.
- Many smokers prefer to have the support of others who are trying to quit and find it helpful to join stop-smoking self-help groups or clinics.

# Smoking Fact Sheet 5

### Tobacco advertising

- Tobacco companies have always spent heavily on advertising their products. Although TV advertising of cigarettes has been banned in the UK for a number of years, until recently there continued to be a great deal of advertising through magazines, newspapers and billboards.
- Tobacco companies have made use of indirect advertising, for example by sponsoring major sports events (e.g. Formula One racing) and brand stretching (applying the tobacco brand and logo to other products such as clothing).
- Advertising creates the effect that smoking is socially acceptable.
- Young people seem to have been particularly influenced by advertising and sports sponsorship to buy those brands that are advertised most heavily[2].
- The tobacco industry has argued that advertising is aimed only at existing smokers, to promote brand loyalty and switching between brands, but there is strong evidence that advertising has encouraged young people to start smoking.
- In 1996 a survey found that 75% of 11- to 16-year-olds could identify at least one sport connected to cigarette advertising through sponsorship[20].
- Since the Government announced its intention to ban tobacco advertising, the tobacco industry has reduced expenditure on advertising and has shifted marketing funds to direct mail advertising, sponsorship, sales promotions and other promotional activities[27].

### The case for banning advertising

- Although TV advertising of cigarettes is banned in the UK, the Government has largely relied on voluntary agreements with the tobacco industry to restrict the impact of advertising on young people.
- The UK Government is now committed to implementing a new EU Directive that will end tobacco sponsorship by July 2003 (2006 in special cases).
- The ban on sponsorship has led many sports to claim that they have had difficulty in finding funds to replace it.
- The Directive still allows advertising in specialist tobacconist shops, under strict control.
- When cigarette advertising was banned in Norway, the number of young people taking up smoking reduced by 50%.
- Over 60% of the British public is in favour of a ban on all tobacco advertising.
- In 1994 the tobacco industry spent an estimated £47.5 million on press advertising[23], £15–20 million on poster advertising[24] and £7.5 million on sponsoring sports events[25].
- In 1994 it is estimated that the industry spent £60–100 million on promotion[5].

### Smoking and the law

- Although it is not against the law for children to smoke, it is illegal to sell cigarettes to anyone under the age of 16.
- Shopkeepers are required to display a sign stating the law on tobacco sales to under 16s and those who do sell illegally can be prosecuted and fined.
- Trading Standards Officers work with young people to check on shopkeepers. These young people are specially selected and trained to go into shops and ask to buy cigarettes.
- In recent years, the Government has demanded that Trading Standards Officers take tougher action against shopkeepers breaking the law. It is argued that young people are more likely to become regular smokers if they find it easy to buy cigarettes.
- Others argue that catching out shopkeepers will not stop young people acquiring cigarettes.
- It is estimated in 1994 that young people spend £135 million on cigarettes, giving £108 million to the Government in tax revenues[22].
- A survey in 1996 found that only 11% of children who had tried to buy cigarettes in a shop were refused the last time they did so and only 3% of 15-year-olds were refused[19].

# References

1. 'Stop smoking products – a quitter's guide.' *Which? Way to Health* February, 1993.
2. ASH (Action on Smoking and Health).
3. US Surgeon General. *The Health Consequences of Smoking: Nicotine Addiction.* (USGPO, 1988)
4. The *UK Smoking Epidemic – Deaths in 1995.* (Health Education Authority, 1998)
5. *Report of the Scientific Committee on Tobacco and Health.* (Department of Health, 1988)
6. Doll, R. *British Medical Journal* 8.10.94 Vol. 309: 901–911.
7. Peto, R. 'Smoking and death: the past 40 years and the next 40'. *British Medical Journal* 1994. 309: 901–911.
8. *Cost Effectiveness of Smoking Cessation Interventions.* (Health Education Authority and Centre for Health Economics, University of York, 1997)
9. House of Commons, Hansard WA Col 327, 4.6.98.
10. House of Commons, Hansard WA Col 465, 8.6.98.
11. *Health Effects of Exposure to Environmental Tobacco Smoke.* Report of the Office of Environmental Health Hazards Assessment. (California, 1997)
12. *Smoking and the Young.* Royal College of Physicians, 1992.
13. Strachan, DP and Cook, DG *Thorax 1997*; 52: 905–914.
14. *Passive Smoking: Summary of New Findings.* (ASH, November 1997)
15. Guardian/OCM opinion poll 13.1.98.
16. *Passive Smoking.* ASH Briefing. (ASH, 1998)
17. *Inkpen Litterbug Report.* (Tidy Britain Group, 1995)
18. *Summary Fire Statistics United Kingdom 1996.* (Home Office, 1998)
19. Office for National Statistics. Jervis L. *Smoking Among Secondary Schoolchildren in 1996: England.* (HMSO, 1997)
20. *MORI Schools Omnibus Survey 1996.*
21. Jarvis M et al. *British Medical Journal* 1985; 291: 927–929.
22. Foulds J *British Medical Journal* 1995; 311: 1152–1153.
23. MEAL, 1994.
24. *Marketing Week* 20.5.94.
25. House of Commons, Hansard Col. 375W, 7.12.95.
26. West R. *Tobacco withdrawal symptoms.* (St George's Hospital Medical School, 1996)
27. 'Stubbing out advertising.' *Marketing Week*, 5.1.96.

# Useful addresses and resources

ASH (Action on Smoking and Health) produce a wide range of information and resources covering all aspects of smoking. All the above references were taken from their website.
Tel: 0171 739 5902   Website: http://www.ash.org.uk

The Health and Safety Executive produce an information leaflet called *Passive smoking in the workplace*.
Tel: 0541 54 55 00

The Public Health Department of your Local Health Authority is a good general resource for materials relating to smoking.

*Smoking Kills: A White Paper on Tobacco.* December 1998. (The Stationery Office, 1998)

Callum C. *The UK Smoking Epidemic: Deaths in 1995.* (Health Education Authority, 1998)

Doll R, Crofton J, eds. *British Medical Bulletin: Tobacco and Health.* (The Royal Society of Medicine Press, 1996; Vol. 52)

Walters R, Whent H. *Health Update: Smoking.* (Health Education Authority, 1996)

# Skills matrix

| ACTIVITY/ SKILL | 1 | 2 | 3 | 4 | 5 | 6 | 7 | 8 | 9 | 10 | 11 | 12 | 13 | 14 | 15 | 16 | 17 | 18 | 19 |
|---|---|---|---|---|---|---|---|---|---|---|---|---|---|---|---|---|---|---|---|
| Analysing/Interpreting | ● | ● | ● | ● | ● | ● | ● | ● | ● | ● | ● | ● | ● | ● | ● | ● | ● | ● | ● |
| Asserting | | | | | | | ● | | | | ● | ● | ● | | ● | | | | |
| Awareness | ● | ● | ● | ● | ● | ● | ● | ● | ● | ● | ● | ● | ● | ● | ● | ● | ● | ● | ● |
| Collating | | | | | | | ● | ● | | | | | ● | ● | | | ● | | |
| Communicating | ● | ● | ● | ● | ● | | ● | ● | ● | ● | ● | ● | ● | ● | ● | ● | ● | ● | ● |
| Comparing | | ● | ● | ● | | | ● | | ● | ● | | | | | | | ● | ● | ● |
| Cooperating | ● | ● | ● | ● | ● | ● | ● | ● | ● | ● | ● | ● | ● | ● | ● | ● | ● | ● | ● |
| Debating and discussing | | ● | ● | ● | ● | ● | ● | ● | ● | ● | ● | ● | | ● | ● | | | ● | ● |
| Decision making | ● | ● | ● | | | ● | ● | ● | | | ● | ● | ● | | | | | | ● |
| Empathising | | | | | | | ● | ● | ● | | | | ● | | ● | ● | ● | | |
| Evaluating | ● | ● | | ● | ● | ● | ● | ● | ● | ● | ● | ● | ● | | ● | ● | ● | ● | ● |
| Expressing (e.g. of beliefs, ideas and opinions) | | ● | ● | ● | ● | | ● | ● | ● | ● | ● | ● | ● | ● | | ● | ● | ● | ● |
| ICT | | | | | | | | | ● | | | ● | | ● | ● | | | | ● |
| Identity and self-esteem | | | | | | | ● | ● | ● | | ● | | | | | | | | ● |
| Imagining | ● | ● | | | ● | | | | ● | | | | ● | | ● | ● | | | |
| Investigating | ● | | | | | | ● | ● | ● | | ● | | | ● | ● | | | | |
| Knowledge | ● | ● | ● | ● | ● | ● | ● | ● | ● | ● | ● | ● | ● | ● | ● | ● | ● | ● | ● |
| Listening | | ● | ● | | ● | ● | ● | ● | ● | | | ● | ● | ● | ● | ● | ● | ● | |
| Negotiating | | | | | | | | | | | | | ● | | | | ● | | |
| Perceiving | ● | | ● | | | ● | ● | ● | | | ● | | ● | | | ● | | | |
| Presenting | ● | | | | | ● | ● | | ● | ● | ● | ● | ● | | ● | | | ● | ● |
| Prioritising | | ● | | | | | | | | ● | | ● | | | | | | | ● |
| Problem solving | | | | | | | | | | ● | | | ● | | | ● | ● | ● | ● |
| Respect | | | | | | | | ● | | | | | | | ● | | | | |
| Responsibility | | ● | ● | | | ● | ● | ● | ● | ● | | | ● | ● | ● | | | ● | ● |
| Understanding | ● | ● | ● | ● | ● | ● | ● | ● | ● | ● | ● | ● | ● | ● | ● | ● | ● | ● | ● |